This book is intended for educational and informational purposes only. It is not a substitute for medical, psychological, or professional advice. Always seek the guidance of a qualified professional regarding any questions about a child's development or mental health.

Illustrations created by the author with the assistance of AI-supported digital tools.
Edited by: Paul MacRae

Independently published.

To my two boys,
May you explore your world with wonder, use your brilliant minds in your own special ways, and always feel brave enough to reach for the stars that light up your sky.
And to my husband, your unconditional love and support helped me believe in myself to write this book.

Love always, Mama

Professional Praise

Orbit Brothers: A Young Explorers Guide to ADHD is a remarkable and uplifting resource for children and families navigating the world of ADHD. Vanessa Fata has created something truly special—a book that is both imaginative and deeply practical. Through the engaging metaphor of space exploration, young readers are guided to better understand their brains, emotions, and strengths, while parents and educators gain valuable insight into how to support them with compassion and curiosity.

Each chapter builds beautifully on the next, transforming complex psychological concepts—like emotional regulation, mindfulness, and executive functioning—into accessible and empowering lessons. I especially appreciate how Vanessa normalizes the challenges associated with ADHD while celebrating the creativity, energy, and innovation that often accompany it.

The "missions" woven throughout the book make learning tangible and fun, helping children develop real-world skills in focus, organization, and problem solving—while reinforcing that their differences are not deficits, but unique gifts to be understood and harnessed.

Orbit Brothers is more than a guide—it's a journey of self-discovery, courage, and confidence. This book will surely become a trusted companion in homes, schools, and clinics alike.

— Dr. Jillian Roberts

Child Psychologist · Professor, University of Victoria · Bestselling Children's Author

Table of Contents

A Note to Parents

Thank you for choosing and reading this book to support your child; it truly matters.

Inside these pages, your young astronaut will learn tools to understand their ADHD brain, and you will gain insight into how they think, feel, and learn best.

This book is more than an activity guide. It's a bridge to help you and your child build stronger habits, better communication, and a shared language for emotions, focus, and confidence.

This is not a book meant to be rushed.
ADHD brains learn best with time, practice, and repetition.
I recommend exploring one chapter at a time, practicing the tool together, and then moving forward when your child feels ready.
Small steps build strong skills.

Colouring Pages Guide

Inside this book, you'll find special space-themed colouring pages.
These aren't just for fun (although they are super fun!); they're part of your astronaut training.
You can use each colouring page as:

A REWARD

Finish a mission? Complete a task?
Colour a page to celebrate your success!

A BREAK

If your brain feels busy, tired, or overwhelmed, take a colouring break to recharge, just as astronauts pause between missions.

A MOTIVATION BOOSTER

Pick a page you want to learn and work toward finishing it one step at a time.

Every page you colour shows how far you've travelled on your learning journey.
So grab your pencils, choose your mission, and get ready to launch!

CHAPTER 1

UNDERSTANDING ADHD & YOUR BRAIN

Your Brain's Spark

ADHD is like having a rocket-ship brain.
Sometimes it zooms really fast, full of energy and ideas.
Other times it drifts off course when you're trying to focus.

Your rocket isn't broken, it just works differently.

Learning how your rocket flies helps you understand your strengths and what tools help you steer your rocket.

ADHD 101

ATTENTION DEFICIT HYPERACTIVE DISORDER

In space terms:

A – Asteroid Attention!
Your focus might bounce from one idea to another..

D – Double the Drive!
You've got big energy and motivation when something excites you.

H – Hyper Booster Mode
Sometimes your engines run too fast, making it hard to stop.

D – Dynamic Dreamer!
You see the universe differently! Full of colour, ideas, and possibilities!

The Captain

Let's talk about something important in ADHD:

Executive Function

Think of your brain as a spaceship, and you are the <u>Captain!</u>

Executive Function is just a fancy way of saying, "The Captain's in charge."

It helps you plan missions, stay focused, remember items, and make good choices.

When you hear "Executive Function," just think:

Captain = YOU!

Unfocused Missions

Even Captains have unfocused days at Mission Control.

That's called **Executive <u>Dysfunction.</u>**
This is when it's hard to steer your spaceship.

Maybe the boosters won't start, the map looks tricky,
or the buttons just won't work!
It can make starting, focusing, or finishing
a mission tricky.

Good news — every astronaut has off days!
With the right tools, helpers, and practice, you can
always get your spaceship back on track.

Control Panel

Let's think of your brain as the main control panel.

Your brain has **3** main control centers that guide your mission:

Cortex
Limbic System
Brain Stem

Here is an easy way to remember them:

Meet Your Brain

CORTEX

The Captain's Control Room

This is the part of your brain that helps you **think**, plan, and make choices.

It helps the Captain (that's you!) solve problems, focus, and use imagination.

This is where smart decisions take flight

LIMBIC SYSTEM

The Guard Robot & Alarm System

This part of your brain handles **feelings** and memories.

Inside it lives the Guard Robot, called the Amygdala.

When something feels big, scary, or surprising, the amygdala turns on the alarm.

It can make you:

- **Fight** – get ready to act
- **Run** – zoom away fast
- **Freeze** – stay still like space ice
- **Please** – try to make things okay

BRAIN STEM

The Ship's Auto-Pilot

This part keeps your spaceship running, even when you're not thinking about it.

It controls breathing, heartbeat, and staying calm or alert.

When your heart races or your body feels shaky, this system helps steady your ship.

SELENA

CHAPTER 2

SELF-ESTEEM & STRENGTHS

Your Superpower

Every astronaut has superpowers.
You are likely creative, funny, kind, brave, or all of these!
Having ADHD can make some missions feel tricky, like staying focused, finishing a task, or remembering your space checklist.
It also gives you incredible strengths that help your rocket shine!

You might find that your brain helps you:

- Think in amazing new ways (great for solving problems!)
- Come up with creative ideas no one else sees
- Notice tiny details others might miss
- Have endless energy for things you love
- Feel deeply and care big about the people and things that matter most to you

The Shine List

Every astronaut has a special light that makes them shine!

On the next page, write or draw three things that you like about yourself.

Maybe you're kind, creative, brave, or funny.
These are "shine traits" that help you glow, even on cloudy days.

Remember, your light makes the universe brighter, just by being you!

The Shine List

List OR draw your shine traits

1. ______________________

2. ______________________

3. ______________________

Self Talk Tips

Spot Your Strengths: Notice what you do well instead of only focusing on what's tricky.

Use Kind Space Talk: Tell yourself things like, "I can try again," or "I'm still learning."

Celebrate Your Brain Power: Remember, your brain is a gift that helps you see things other explorers might miss!

Your Orbit Strengths

Find your Orbit Strengths

Gizmo says:
"Write three ways your brain helps each day! See my examples below..."

- I have awesome ideas.
- I care about my friends.
- I never give up.

Your turn!

1. ____________________
2. ____________________
3. ____________________

Star Care Week

It's Star Care Week, when all astronauts help dim stars to regain their sparkle. Leo and Vince are excited to help. They meet Luna, a little star who's lost her glow — they realize it's not a broken lightbulb...
it's low self-esteem.

Luna says, "I'm not bright like the other stars. I just make the sky look crowded."

Vince tries to cheer her up with silly jokes, but it doesn't work...

Leo, frustrated, sighs,
"Maybe she just needs more stardust!"
and goes searching.

Then Selena reminds them gently,
"Stars don't shine brighter because of dust...
they shine when they remember who they are."

She teaches Luna and the boys about positive self-talk and seeing strengths instead of flaws.

Together, they build Gizmo's "Shine Reflector," a mirror that only shows the good things that you say about yourself.

When Luna finally says:

The mirror glows, and so does she.

CHAPTER 3

SELF-AWARENESS

What is Self-Awareness?

Self-awareness means noticing what's happening **inside you and around you.**

Your body and brain send clues all the time. **Self-awareness** is learning how to spot those clues.

Noticing doesn't mean something is wrong...
It doesn't mean you have to fix anything...
It just means you're paying attention.

Clues are information!

Body & Brain Clues

Your body and brain send you clues that help you learn more about yourself.

These clues can look like:

BODY CLUES

- Wiggly hands or feet
- Tight shoulders
- A fast heartbeat
- Tired eyes
- A heavy or buzzy feeling

These clues aren't bad.
They're your body sharing information.

Your body is saying.
"Something is changing."

BRAIN CLUES

- Thoughts racing
- Getting stuck on one idea
- Wanting to quit suddenly
- Feeling overwhelmed
- Feeling done or foggy

These thoughts aren't trouble.
They're signals.
Your brain is saying.

"Something is happening."

Why Noticing Matters

The earlier you notice a clue,
the more choices you have later.

If you notice **early**,
you can decide what you need next.
If you notice **late**,
things can feel louder or harder.

That's why grown-ups help kids practice noticing.
Not to change you,
but to help you understand yourself.

Self-awareness gives you information, not rules.

Gizmo's Reminders

Sometimes you just notice:

"My body feels different."

"My brain is getting loud."

"This feels harder than before."

That's enough.

Noticing is the first step.

What you do next comes later.

CHAPTER 4

EMOTIONAL REGULATION

Feelings Control Panel

The BIG word for controlling your feelings is called,

EMOTIONAL REGULATION.

Imagine your feelings as a colourful button on your spaceship's control panel.

Self-Regulating

Sometimes the red button might flash when you feel anger, frustration, or even big excitement.

When you notice a button glowing, you can pause, take a breath, and decide what to do next.
That's you using your Emotional Regulation skills, like a captain bringing their ship back to a steady course.

- Taking deep breaths
- Moving your body
- A quick break

Next, let's dive into an example in a short story...

Captain Vince and His Spark

Astronaut Vince and his robot buddy Gizmo, zoomed through the stars in their silver rocket.

They were heading to Volcano Planet to collect glowing moon rocks.

When they landed, BOOM!

The ground shook and hot lava bubbled nearby.

Vince's heart raced; his red light flashed!

"We have to go home! Now!" he shouted.

Gizmo blinked his big, white eyes.
"Breathe, Vince. In... and out."

Vince crossed his arms.
"But, I'm scared!"
Vince's red light was still flashing...

"That's okay," said Gizmo.
"Scared feelings are like space dust.
Let's float through them!"

Vince took a deep breath,
then another. His hands stopped shaking.

He looked around and noticed that the lava was far away now.

"It's not so scary when I breathe", he said. Vince's red light was now yellow...

Gizmo smiled.
"Exactly! Feelings don't last forever... just like space storms!"

Together, they collected the glowing moon rocks and then blasted off into the calm, starry sky.

Emotional Regulation

Take big breaths in and out
to calm down.

CHAPTER 5

WORRY

What is Worry?

You learned how to calm your body and mind.
Amazing job, astronaut!

Now it's time to learn what to do when worries show up.

- Every astronaut worries sometimes, even the bravest captains in the galaxy, and that's okay.
- Worries can pop up at school, at bedtime, or even during fun moments.
- They might make your brain feel full, your tummy feel tight, or your thoughts feel a little funky.
- The important part is noticing the worry... and then, sending it back into space so you can stay calm, focused, and enjoy your day.

MUNCH

Meet Munch. Munch is a silly, friendly, worry-eating monster who LOVES to munch on kid worries from galaxies far and near.

Together, you'll explore different worry tools and pick the strategies that feel best for you.
And remember, you can use any worry tool, any time, on any mission!

Feed Your Worries

Here is your first tool to try:

The Munch Monster Box is a decorated tissue box that becomes your worry helper.

You can paint it, wrap it, glue eyes on it, add cardboard teeth, stickers, stars, glitter, anything you like! The more creative and silly, the better.

This "monster" has a special job:
It eats your worries so YOU don't have to hold them.

When you feed your worries to the monster, your brain gets lighter and calmer, just like clearing junk out of your rocket before blastoff.

Monster Steps

1. **Create and name your monster:**
Decorate the tissue box into a monster. Give your monster a name like, "Captain Crunch".

2. **Write down your worry on a small piece of paper:**
You can draw it if that's easier.

3. **Feed the monster your worry through its mouth:**
CHOMP! CHOMP! CHOMP!

Your monster eats the worry so you don't have to now.

4. **Take a deep space breath IN... 3...2...1...**
Breath OUT and imagine your monster blasting the worry into space.

5. **Close the mission:**
"Worry handled, mission complete!"

Worry Scanner

Mission: Scan It Like Gizmo the Robot!

1. Pretend you have a space scanner (your finger).
2. "Scan" your body from your head to toes.
3. When you find a "worry spot" (tight chest, tummy feeling weird), put your hand on it.
4. Hold your palm over the worry spot, close your eyes, and take 5 slow breaths to help it relax.
5. Shake the worries off and try to continue with what you were doing!

Worry Talk Through

Mission: Call Mission Control!

Tell a trusted adult your worry. They are your "Mission Control".

Mission Control helps you think of safe, smart next steps.

When you talk it out, the worry shrinks like a tiny fading star.

Blasting Through Worries

One afternoon, Leo and Vince were getting ready for a new space mission.
Leo checked the control panel carefully, but something didn't feel right.

His thoughts felt noisy... like too many radios playing at once.

Vince bounced beside him, but even he was quieter than usual.

"My tummy feels funny," Vince said. "What if I mess up the mission?"

Leo took a slow breath.
"I think we're feeling... worried," he said.

The stars around them flickered softly.
And that's when they heard a gentle munch... munch... munch...

From behind a moon hopped a small, round creature with big eyes and tiny teeth.

"Hi!" said Munch. "I'm a worry helper."

Leo knelt down. "Do you eat worries?"

Munch smiled wide. "Only the ones you're ready to let go of."

Vince held his hands close to his chest. "My worry feels big," he whispered.

"That's okay," Munch said gently. "You don't have to push it away... Just notice it."

Leo closed his eyes for a moment. "I notice my worry is telling me I have to be perfect," he said.
Munch nodded. "That's a tired worry."
Crunch.

Vince giggled as Munch crunched a little more.
"My worry feels smaller now," he said.
"Not gone... just quieter."
Leo smiled. "Mine too."

Munch wiped his mouth and sat beside them.
"Worries like to visit," he said.
"But you don't have to carry them alone."

The stars glowed brighter as the mission screen lit up.
Leo stood tall. "Ready, Captain Vince?"
Vince nodded.
"With Munch," he said, "I think we can handle this."

And together, they blasted off... worries and all!

CHAPTER 6

UNDERSTANDING IMPULSIVITY

Impulsivity 101

Sometimes your brain zooms into Blast-Off Mode before you've had time to think or make a plan. This is called impulsivity, and many astronauts with ADHD experience it, even the best captains in the galaxy!

Think of impulsivity like having super-speed booster rockets on your spaceship.

These boosters can be awesome when you need creativity, bravery, or quick action, but sometimes they fire at the wrong moment, sending you flying into a mission before you're ready.

Good News, Astronaut...

Your rocket isn't broken, it just has super-boosters. And super-boosters don't need fixing. They need training, practice, and the right tools, just like real astronauts use in space.

Blast-Off Brain

Here are some ways your brain might be feeling when it blasts off too soon, before your mission.

- Interrupting without meaning to
- Acting before thinking (running, shouting, grabbing, jumping)
- Rushing and making mistakes
- Saying something fast, then wishing you hadn't
- Having trouble waiting or taking turns
- Starting a mission without checking the steps first

Try these tools...

1 Freeze the Boosters!

If you want to grab, touch, poke, or move:

Put your hands behind your back or in your pockets and whisper:

"Hands to space."

This helps your boosters from acting out too fast.

2 Gizmo's Scan

Pretend Gizmo is standing beside you saying:

"Captain, let's scan before we act!"

Imagine scanning your brain like a robot:

Beep...boop...

Is this a good time to act or talk?

These tools help you slow your boosters, take a breath, and choose your next move, even when your brain wants to zoom ahead!

Stop-See-Choose

STOP— Pause your body
(Freeze! Hands to yourself. Feet still.)

SEE— Look at...

- What's happening?
- What am I feeling?
- What could happen next, if I react?

CHOOSE— Pick your best next move:

- A safe choice
- A kind choice
- A helpful choice
- A mission-smart choice

Use your orbit tool any time you feel rushed, grabby, or reckless!

Comet Canyon

Leo, Vince, Selena, and Gizmo were exploring Comet Canyon, a glowing place full of sparkling space crystals.

"Look at all those treasures!" Leo shouted, zooming ahead.

"Leo, wait!" Selena called, but Leo's boosters were already firing.

ZOOM!
He grabbed a crystal, pressed a blinking button, and...

BOOOOP!
A giant bubble shield popped up around him, trapping him inside!

Leo bounced off the bubble walls.
"Uh-oh... I didn't mean to do that."

Gizmo rolled over, blinking.
"Captain Leo, your boosters fired too fast.
Let's run a Boosters Check!"

Selena nodded.
"Remember the trick?
STOP-SEE-CHOOSE!"

Leo froze like space ice.
He looked around... SEE.

He took a breath,
and said,
"I choose to ask for help."
Vince grinned.

"Great choice, Leo!
Now let's pop this bubble."

Together, they pressed the release panel.
POP! The bubble vanished.

Leo brushed space dust off of his suit.
"My boosters were too fast," he said.
"Next time, I'll try a 3-Second Space Pause."

Selena smiled.
"See? Even captains need practice steering their rockets."

The crew continued their adventure, this time with Leo steering his boosters like a true space captain.

Interrupting

Oops! My Rocket Blasted Off!

Sometimes your words blast out of your mouth super fast before your brain even knows what happened!

This is called **interrupting**, and lots of astronauts with ADHD experience it.
It doesn't mean you're rude, it means your brain rockets are extra speedy.

Interrupting can happen when:

1. You're excited
2. You have a great idea

3. You're worried you'll forget what you want to say
4. Your brain is going too fast

Comet Catch

The Comet Catch Technique

When a thought zooms in fast (like a comet), catch it before it crashes out of your mouth.

Steps:

1. Pretend you're grabbing a comet in your hand.
2. Close your fist gently.
3. Hold it until the person finishes speaking.
4. When it's your turn, open your hand and "release" your comet thought.

Why it works:

It keeps your thought safe so your brain doesn't panic and interrupt.

CHAPTER 7

WORKING MEMORY

Working Memory

REMEMBER: Working memory is what your brain holds onto right now so you can finish a mission.

Astronauts use working memory all the time. It helps them remember what they're doing, what step comes next, and which tool they're using.

Kids with ADHD can have a tricky working memory. Their brain "backpack" may drop things while they're using them. It's not because they aren't trying, but because their brain is processing a lot at once.

Think of working memory like a tiny astronaut backpack. It carries only what you need right now, like:

- What you're doing
- Your current step
- Directions you're following
- The tool you're using
- What you're working on

If your backpack gets too full, things can fall out before you even start!

That's when working memory tools can help.

Memory Glitch

WHOOPS!

Out falls the homework page, or the instructions, or the directions you were just told.

Here's what a Working Memory Glitch might look like on your mission:

- You forget step-by-step instructions.
- You walk into a room and forget why.
- You start a task... then float away to something else.
- You lose track of tools (pencils, books, etc.).
- You forget what you were about to say.
- You reread the same line over and over.

Moon Steps

Astronauts don't take giant leaps during missions, they take Moon Steps!

This tool helps you remember each step of a task so that your backpack doesn't overflow.

Why It Works

1. Break your task into 3 Moon Steps
   a. You can draw moons or number each step
2. Say them out loud
   "Step 1: Put books away, step 2: Pack lunch, step 3: Zip backpack."
3. Touch each finger as you say each step
4. This anchors the steps into the brain.
5. After each step, check it off with a star, sticker, or space symbol.

Why It Works

Working memory is stronger when information is spoken, seen, and touched.

Gizmo Repeats

Gizmo's Repeat-Back Rule

Featuring Gizmo, the Robot!

Gizmo is great at remembering things because he always repeats instructions out loud.

How It Works:

1. Look at the person (or pretend to look at Gizmo!)
2. Repeat the direction back:
   a: "Okay! You want me to put my socks on and bring my water bottle."
3. Start the mission
4. Gizmo Check:
   a: Ask yourself, "Does Gizmo say I did everything?"

Why It Works:

Repeating directions sends the information into your "longer-lasting" memory file.

Selena's Memory Glitch

Selena floated into the hallway of the Space Station, humming.
Today was her turn to prep the ship for launch.

"Selena," Mission Control said,
"Please gather the tools,
check the fuel,
and turn on the navigation lights."

She saluted.
"On it!"
She zoomed down the hall...
and then stopped.

"What was I supposed to do again?" she wondered.

Her brain backpack had dropped the steps!
Just then, Gizmo rolled up beside her.

"Beep! Captain Selena, try my Repeat-Back Rule!"

Selena closed her eyes.
"Okay...
Step 1: Gather tools.
Step 2: Check fuel.
Step 3: Lights!"

"Excellent recall!" Gizmo cheered.
Selena smiled.

"I remembered! Let's launch!"

And together, they blasted off...

CHAPTER 8

FORGETFULNESS

Forgetfulness

Do you ever forget homework, plans, or something on your mission list?

Forgetfulness is a tricky brain skill, and it's very common for kids with ADHD.

Sometimes your brain hears something important...
but it doesn't get saved for later.

That doesn't mean you didn't care.
It just means your brain didn't store it in time.

Just like space, this challenge can feel big.

But here's the good news:
Forgetfulness isn't something that disappears,
it's something you learn to manage.
And there are tools that help you
catch important thoughts before they
float away.

What It Can Look Like...

Forgetfulness can show up in different ways.
Sometimes it looks like:

- Leaving homework at home
- Missing an activity or appointment
- Forgetting a playdate
- Not telling someone something important
- Missing a deadline

You might think,
"I'll remember later."
But later comes... and the thought is gone and forgotten.

This doesn't happen because you're careless.
It happens because thoughts need a safe place to stay.

Distractions Are Louder

Distractions are louder

Everyone gets distracted.
But ADHD brains notice more things.

- ✔ Sounds
- ✔ Movements
- ✔ Ideas
- ✔ Feelings

When something new grabs your attention, your brain may switch directions quickly.
The first thought doesn't disappear on purpose.
It just loses its spot.

Forgetting is not laziness.
Your brain just works a little differently.
And every brain can learn tools to help it stay on course.

Why Thoughts Slip Away

The "Holding Area" in Your Brain

At the front of your brain is a part called the **Prefrontal Cortex.**

Its job is to:

- ✔ Hold thoughts
- ✔ Remember steps
- ✔ Finish what you start
- ✔ Ignore distractions

In ADHD brains, this area is still growing and doesn't always hold thoughts very strongly.
So sometimes...
A thought fades before you're done using it because the signal wasn't strong enough.

Dopamine

Your Brain's "Power Booster"

Your brain cells use tiny chemical messengers to talk with each other.
One important one is called **Dopamine.**

Dopamine helps:

- ✔ Keep thoughts "on"
- ✔ Make your focus stronger
- ✔ Boost important signals

In ADHD, dopamine can be lower or harder to use.
That means thoughts don't stay powered up for long.

But when something feels interesting or exciting, the brain can make more dopamine.
That's why ADHD brains can focus really well on things that they love.

It's like a flashlight with weak batteries...
until something exciting gives it a boost.
Then the light shines brighter again.

The Rule

When something pops into your head
that you'll need later,
there is one important rule:
Write it down right away.

Thoughts don't wait.
Writing it down gives your brain
a safe place to put the idea.
Your brain doesn't have to hold onto it anymore.
It can relax, knowing it's been saved.
Writing things down isn't extra work.
It's how you protect important ideas
before they disappear.

On the next page,
you'll use the Space Junk Master List
to catch your thoughts
the moment they appear.
Later, we'll learn how to sort them.

Space Junk Master List

FIRST!

Write all of your space junk below:

Leo's Thoughts Floated Away

One morning, Leo had a lot on his mind.
A library book to return.
A playdate to remember.
A question he wanted to ask at dinner.
The thoughts popped into his head like little stars.
Bright and important.
But Leo kept going.
"I'll remember later," he thought.
As the day zoomed by, the stars began to drift.
One floated past lunchtime.
Another slipped away during soccer.
By bedtime, the sky felt quiet.
Leo frowned.
"Where did my thoughts go?"

Gizmo floated closer and smiled.
"When thoughts don't have a place to land," he said,
"they sometimes drift away."
Leo grabbed his Space Junk Master List.
As soon as a thought popped up,
he gave it a safe place to stay.
The stars stopped drifting.
They stayed right where Leo could find them.
Leo felt lighter.
His brain could relax.
And that night, as Leo looked up at the stars,
he knew exactly where his important thoughts were waiting.

Space Junk
Master List
Test moon boots
Galaxy class at 4PM
Collect asteoid
rocks.
LEO

CHAPTER 9

FOCUS & ATTENTION

WHEN THE CONTROLS GET WIGGLY

What Focus Feels Like With ADHD

Every astronaut's brain works a little differently.

For kids with ADHD, focus can feel tricky and wiggly, like trying to steer a spaceship while lots of things are happening at once.

- Sometimes your brain might jump from thought to thought, even when you want to pay attention.
- Sometimes your body might want to move, even when you're sitting still.
- Getting started can be the hardest part, even when you know what to do. Once you begin, it can feel easier to keep going.
- Noises, lights, and movement might feel extra loud, like everything is calling for your attention at the same time.

This doesn't mean you're not trying.
It just means your brain needs fuel and support to stay on course.

When Focus Feels Tricky

Circle anything that feels tricky for you.
It doesn't have to happen every day, just sometimes.
Next, we'll learn why these things happen and what can help.

- Difficulty starting tasks
- Difficulty ignoring any or all distractions
- Poor time management
- Difficulty staying focused and shifting focus
- Procrastination Avoiding tasks
- Burnout; Lack of motivation, Overwhelmed
- Difficulty managing emotions or behaviors

Why Focus Can Feel Hard

The Struggle to Focus

Sometimes, focusing can be tough, especially for kids with ADHD. That's because your brain gets distracted by a lot of different signals all at once, like thoughts, noises, and movement. These signals can pull you away from your work without you even noticing!

Your Attention Span

Everyone's attention span is different, and it can change depending on how interesting something is, how tired you are, and how long you've been trying to focus.

Think of it like a gauge:

- How interesting a task is.
- Your energy (how tired or awake you feel).
- How long you've been trying to focus.

Focus Fuel Tank

Every astronaut has a "focus fuel tank."
The older you get, the more focus fuel you can carry!

Scientists on Earth say that most kids can stay focused for about 2–3 minutes for each year of their age.

An Example:

A 6-year-old astronaut might focus for 12–18 minutes before needing a quick space stretch.
A 10-year-old might last 20–30 minutes!

Based on the information provided, what is your attention span?

Motivation

Every astronaut needs fuel to blast off.
Your brain works the same way!

Inside your mind, there is something called the Reward Pathway. It's like the fuel tank that powers your focus, energy, and excitement.

But guess what?

Astronauts with ADHD have special rockets that don't always turn on with boring, slow, or tricky missions.

Your Rocket LOVES:

- Start something excitedly... then drift away
- Have a hard time returning to a half-finished mission
- Forget what you are doing
- Get distracted by something more fun
- Feel bored quickly
- Need reminders or boosters to finish tasks

Spark Fuel

Spark Fuel is the brain energy that helps you start.
ADHD brains sometimes wait for
interest to create fuel.

But here is a secret astronauts learn:
Starting creates **Spark Fuel.**
Even small starts can wake up your rocket.
When you try a tool, your brain begins
to build focus energy.
That energy is your **Spark Fuel.**

Try a familiar tool, like:

 Freeze the boosters

 Rocket Breathing
(Quickly peek at page 92)

 Stop-See-Choose

Every time you try, you earn **Spark Fuel** stars.
And when you collect enough **Spark Fuel**...
your rocket is ready for launch!

Background Boost

Gentle background sounds can help your brain focus!

Some brains focus better when there's just a **little something** extra happening.

⭐ A Background Boost is:

- Something that keeps part of your brain busy
- So the "rest" can focus better!

⭐ Choose one to keep your brain on track:

Calm music

A quiet, familiar show or movie

Songs you already know

White noise, rain, or gentle sounds

NOT a background boost:
Anything that makes you want to **watch,** sing along, or stop your work!

⭐ This isn't distraction — you're refueling!

Astro Sprints; How to:

Astro Sprints are short bursts of focus time, just like a rocket blasting off into space.

You set a timer, work hard until the timer ends, then take a break to recharge your brain!

How to use Astro Sprints:

1. Choose a task: homework, cleaning your room, reading, etc.
2. Set a timer, work hard until it rings!
3. Take a break for 5-10 minutes.
   Stretch, walk, or grab a snack!
4. Repeat! Try to complete 2-4 Astro Sprints.

MISSION REMINDER:

Attention spans come in short bursts!

That's why Astro Sprints are short + powerful.

This idea comes from something called the **Pomodoro Technique**, but we've turned it into a space mission just for you!

Chunking Tasks

Breaking down tasks makes big jobs feel less overwhelming!

When you split a big task into smaller pieces, it's easier to handle and less scary.

- You can focus on one small task at a time and feel proud when you finish each part!
- Stay organized and know what to do next.
- Take breaks and celebrate after finishing a chunk!

Break down a big task...

1. Pick up toys
2. Put dirty clothes in hamper
3. Make bed

LEO
VINCE
15:00

CHAPTER 10

MINDFULNESS TOOLS

Mindfulness

Mindfulness is a superpower every astronaut needs.
It means paying attention to right now; your thoughts, your feelings, your body, and what's happening around you.
Think of mindfulness like turning on your Space Helmet Light.
When the light is on, you can see clearly:
What you're doing
How you're feeling
What your next mission step is
Without it, your brain might zoom into hyper-speed, drift off like space dust.

Mindfulness helps astronauts:

- Slow down racing thoughts
- Calm big feelings
- Focus on one mission at a time
- Feel more in control of their rocket

Rocket Breathing

Even the Orbit Crew uses mindfulness on every adventure...

Leo uses it to stop and breathe.
Selena uses it to calm big feelings.
Vince uses it to stay focused on tricky missions.
And Luna the star guides everyone back to "right now."
Mindfulness is about noticing and choosing your next move with a steady, calm captain inside your brain.

Try Rocket Breathing First:

- Pretend your hands are rocket engines.
- Breathe in through your nose as you "fuel up,"
- Breathe out through your mouth as you "blast off," raising your arms slowly.

REPEAT 3 TIMES

Why it works:

Movement helps you stay FOCUSED.
Breathing slows your body and mind down.

Space Sound

Focus and Awareness

Sit still like an astronaut listening in space...

Close your eyes and name 3 things you can hear (the hum of lights, a clock tick, your breath).

After 30 seconds, open your eyes and say one word to describe how you feel.

Why it works:

It shifts attention from thoughts to sounds, grounding and calming without pressure.

Five Finger Countdown

Hold up one hand.
Touch each finger while saying:

"Breathe in."

"Breathe out."

"Notice what I see."

"Notice what I feel."

"I'm okay now."

Why it works:

The rhythm and touch help your brain focus, steady your zooming thoughts, and bring your feelings back to calm mode (green light).

Thought Log

A Thought Log is like your astronaut notebook for the mind.

- When you feel upset or stressed, you can write down what you're thinking, just like recording space notes during a mission.

- It helps you catch your thoughts. Some thoughts boost your mission (green light), and others can make steering your ship feel really hard (red light).

When you notice a thought that feels hard, you can choose to change course and think in a way that helps you feel calm and focused again.

Then you can try the next tool.

Space Thoughts Record

SITUATION:

What were you doing?

FEELINGS:

What signals did your body send to you during this moment?

BEHAVIOURS:

What did you do OR how did you react when you experienced this?

THOUGHTS:

What thoughts or images were in your mind when you experienced this?

Mindfulness
LEO
VINCE

CHAPTER 11

PROBLEM SOLVING

FIXING THE SPACESHIP

Problem Solving

Troubleshooting Your Spaceship

Sometimes, problems are like spaceship glitches. Maybe a button doesn't work, or your rocket drifts off course. Instead of giving up, astronauts fix the problem step by step.

Problem solving means:

- Slowing down
- Thinking of different options
- Choosing the best one for your mission

Choosing What To Do First

Sometimes we get pulled toward the fun or easy jobs on our list.
They might feel good to do, but they don't always help us finish our big mission goals.
That's why we don't stop at writing things down.
Once your space junk is safely written on your Space Junk Master List, the next step is choosing what to do first.
That's where the 3–2–1 Mission Star System comes in.

First, use your Space Junk Master List
to write down every task floating around in your brain:
big jobs, little jobs, and even the random ones.
Next, sort each task using the:

3–2–1 Mission Star System

- 3 stars = super important (do first!)
- 2 stars = important, but can wait a bit
- 1 star = not urgent (can do later)

When we sort our space junk this way,
it's like building a mission map that helps us decide what to do first
so our space adventure doesn't drift off course!

Space Junk Master List

FIRST!

Write all of your space junk below:

Mission Star Sorting Chart

3

EXAMPLE

- Brush my teeth
- Get dressed
- Tidy my room

2

- Tidy Desk
- Finish 3 questions in math
- Help set the table

1

- Colour a space picture
- Help Mom garden
- Play with toys

Mission Star Sorting Chart

3

2

1

Brainstorm Your Tools

Choose some tools that can help you start and stay focused on a task.

- Astro Sprints
- To do List
- Noise-cancelling headphones
- Focus music: White noise or music
- 1 fidget tool
- Space Junk Master List
- Mission Star Sorting Chart

Write them on the below line

Weekly Schedule

Monday

Tuesday

Wednesday

Thursday

Friday

Saturday

Sunday

Note

Try this chart to help organize your week!

+XP
VINCE

CHAPTER 12

GAMIFYING

In the last chapter,
we learned something
important:

Some missions feel exciting right away...
...and some missions need a little help
to get started.

That's because your rocket runs on
Spark Fuel.

When a mission feels boring,
slow, or tricky,
your fuel tank might stay low,
even if you want to try.

That's where **Mission Mode** comes in.

Mission Mode helps you turn everyday tasks
into something your brain can engage with...

Mission Mode

Mission Mode is not:

- ❌ Forcing yourself
- ❌ Being “good”
- ❌ Finishing perfectly

Mission Mode is about:

- ⭐ Adding fuel
- ⭐ Waking up your reward pathway
- ⭐ Helping your brain stay interested

Games aren’t cheating.
Games are fuel.

Mission Mode means:

- ✅ Turning a task into a game that your brain wants to play.
- ✅ Stay focused
- ✅ Keep going
- ✅ Finish tricky missions

Mission Mode Builder

How the Mission Mode Builder Works

1 What's the Mission?

Name the task like a space mission.

Examples:

- Clean-Up Countdown
- Homework Launch
- Sock Collection Quest

2 Add Spark Fuel (Choose 1 or 2)

This helps activate your reward pathway.

- **A timer** ("Let's play for 5 minutes, then start")
- **Music** or a background Boost
- **Spark Fuel for trying**
  A tool you already learned for focus

Fuel comes before effort – not after.

Your job is not to be perfect.

Your job is to keep your rocket fueled.

Mission Mode Con't'd

3 Play the Mission

- Start small.
- You don't have to finish.
- Stopping is allowed.

Starting = success.

4 Celebrate the Fuel

If you:

✓ Started
✓ Tried
✓ Used a tool
✓ Came back after drifting

That earns **Spark Fuel.**

Not finishing **does not** cancel your fuel.

Your job is **not** to be perfect.

Your job is to keep your rocket **fueled.**

Gamify!
VINCE
SELENA
Spark Fuel

CHAPTER 13

CLASSROOM TRICKS

Classroom Tricks

By now, you know your brain pretty well.
You know it moves fast.
You know thoughts pop in and out.
And you know it works best
with the right kind of help.

School has lots of remembering.
Lots of listening.
Lots of doing the next step.

So instead of trying harder and feeling tired or frustrated...
we use tricks.

Smart astronauts don't rely on memory alone.
They use tools that keep their mission on track.

On the next pages,
you'll learn classroom tricks
that help your brain succeed.

Teacher Talk

Children often freeze when overwhelmed. Give them these helpful scripts to use in class with their teachers:

If confused:

"I don't understand this part.
Can You show me the first step?"

If stuck:

"My brain is overloaded.
Can I take a 1-minute break?"

If anxious:

"My rocket is shaking inside.
Can I breathe for a moment?"

If frustrated:

"I'm overheating.
Can we reset the plan?

These scripts empower children to advocate for themselves. Teachers respect that.

Classroom Tools

These are small things that help your rocket stay steady during school missions:

Tool	What it Means
	Choose a desk that's away from doors, windows, or the "busy galaxy" of the classroom.
Mission Music	Quiet white noise or focus music (if allowed) can help block distractions.
The Silent Signal 	Create a nonverbal signal with your teacher, like raising two fingers, touching your ear, or tapping your desk, to show you need a small break or help staying on track.
Desk Tools 	A quiet fidget, a texture strip taped to your desk, or a wiggle cushion can help your focus boosters stay calm.

Space Station

Desk Organization: Space Station Setup

A messy desk = asteroid field.
A tidy desk = smooth launch.

Top Zone:	Middle Zone	Side Zone
Notebook, pencil	Assignment you're working	Water bottle, quiet fidget

You can even add a small desk checklist.

4 Movement Passes

Movement helps reset your Focus Fuel Tank.

Example:

- 1-minute robot walk
- Bathroom pass
- Water refill mission
- Stretch break (Touch the Stars)

Children with ADHD need movement to regulate, and teachers appreciate simple systems.

Leo's Classroom Lesson

Leo sat at his space desk in Earth School.
The teacher placed a math sheet on his table.

His thoughts zoomed.
The numbers looked huge.
The room felt loud.
His rocket was wobbling.

Selena leaned over
and whispered,
"Use your School
Tools!
What's your first
step?"

Leo took a small
Five Finger Countdown breath.

Then he raised his hand and said,
"Mission Control, I need help with Step One."

The teacher smiled.
Together they solved the first question.

That tiny launch helped Leo fly through the
whole mission smoothly!

MRS
LEO

CHAPTER 14

SOCIAL SKILLS

Crewmates in Space

Astronauts don't fly alone, they work in space crews. Being part of a team means taking turns, listening, and sharing ideas. Sometimes astronauts disagree, but they solve problems together.

Learning social skills helps you build strong friendships and be a great teammate on your crew.

Let's jump into a lesson story next...

Friendships in Space

Making friends is a little like flying a spaceship, too...
Sometimes the journey feels smooth and fun.
Other times, it can feel confusing, bumpy, or even lonely.

Astronauts with ADHD may experience friendship challenges, not because anything is wrong with them, but because their brains work fast, like super-boosters!

Some astronauts find that their super-boost brain creates challenges like:

- Talking over others by accident
- Big feelings in small moments
- Trouble reading social cues
- High energy, a low stop button
- Feeling left out or misunderstood

These challenges don't mean you're a bad friend, they mean your brain is powerful, and learning to steer it helps you connect better with your crew.

Pause Tool

PAUSE:

Pretend you press a glowing button on your space suit.

ORBIT: Float your thought in a tiny circle in your mind.

ASK: "Do I talk now, or wait my turn?"

This gives your brain a few seconds to stop, slow down, and think about your thoughts

Space Team Mission

Leo floated in his space bunk.
Outside the window, stars sparkled.
Below, Earth glowed like a nightlight.

"One day," Leo whispered,
"I'll be the best astronaut in the galaxy. Maybe even the captain!"

BEEP!
The speaker crackled.
"Junior Crew, report to Bay 3!"

Leo grinned.
"A mission! I'm ready!"
He zipped into his suit and pushed off the wall.

WHEEEE! He zoomed down the hallway.

On the moon base, the team had a mission.
Build a shelter before a solar storm hits!

"We need to work together,"
said Vince.

"Let's make a plan," said Selena.

But Leo was already moving.

"I've got this!" he shouted.

He grabbed all the parts.
He started building fast... too fast.

The shelter wobbled.
It tipped...
It tumbled into a pile.

BZZZT! The warning lights flashed.

The "solar storm" was coming!

Selena looked at the mess.
Vince crossed his arms.

"You didn't wait," said Vince.

"You didn't let us help," said Selena.

Leo looked down. "I just wanted to be good," he said. "I wanted to be fast... and helpful."

LEO
SELENA
VINCE

CHAPTER 15

YOUR SLEEP BATTERY

Sleeping is Important!

Every astronaut, including Leo, Vince, Selena, Gizmo, and YOU, need a fully charged Space Battery to launch into a new day.

Sleep is what powers that battery back up.

But with ADHD, drifting off can feel like trying to land a rocket on a bouncing asteroid.

Your brain keeps zooming with ideas, plans, and imagination long after your body is ready for bed.

Here's what that might look like:

- Your body feels wiggly
- You feel "not tired" even though you are
- You lie in bed but your mind blasts off into adventures
- You fall asleep late or wake up early
- You want to get up to play, snack, or explore
- Your brain keeps thinking and thinking

Many space explorers have busy brains, and together we'll help your rocket settle into a soft landing.

Moon Gravity Breathing

Lie in your bed and pretend the moon is gently pulling you down with soft gravity.

Breathe in slowly through your nose.
Breathe out through your mouth and imagine your arms and legs sinking into your bed.

Whisper in your mind:

"Heavy arms..."
"Heavy legs..."
"Heavy body..."

Repeat until your body feels still and calm.

Why it works:

When your body feels heavy, your brain gets the messge: Time to sleep, captain.

Star Shutdown Routine

Astronauts always follow the same shutdown routine so their rockets power off smoothly.

Here is a nightly routine you can follow:

Pick 3-5 calming steps, such as:

- Stretch like a sleepy astronaut
- Brush teeth
- Fill water
- Write or draw 1 thought in your Space Log
- Turn lights low
- Lay down and breathe slow
- Think about a calm place in space

Your brain loves patterns.

Routines = **fewer nighttime zoomies + easier falling asleep.**

Sleep well, Leo

Leo floated in his bunk, staring out
at the stars.
Everyone else was sound asleep:
Vince snored softly, Selena hugged Luna the
star, and Gizmo powered down
with a gentle "beep..."
But Leo's brain?
ZOOM!
WHIRRRR!
PEW-PEW!
He imagined building a mega-ship...
flying to Saturn...
inventing a snack machine that shoots
marshmallows...

"I can't sleep!" Leo groaned.
"My rocket won't power down!"
Gizmo powered up his eyes and rolled over.
"Captain Leo," Gizmo said, "your space battery needs charging for tomorrow's mission."
"I know," Leo said, "but my mind won't stop thinking."
Gizmo beeped kindly.
"That's okay. Many astronauts need help slowing down. Try these tools with me."

First, Gizmo guided Leo through moon gravity breathing until Leo's body felt heavy as if he was sinking into soft moon dust.

Then he started a Star Shutdown Routine,
doing the same steps he does every night:
stretch... sip water... journal...
lights down... deep breaths.
Slowly...
his thoughts softened...
his eyes grew heavy...
and his rocket finally powered down.
When Leo woke up the next morning, he felt
recharged and ready for adventure.
"Sleep really does help,"
he said, stretching.
Gizmo winked.
"Every astronaut needs a full
Space Battery."

Sleep isn't just "rest..."
Sleep gives you:

- ⭐ More focus
- ⭐ Stronger emotional control
- ⭐ Better memory
- ⭐ More creativity
- ⭐ More energy for missions
- ⭐ More patience for tricky moments

When your space battery is charged,

you can handle anything the galaxy sends your way.

ZZZZ

CONGRATULATIONS!

You've travelled through feelings, focus, and self-awareness with Leo, Vince, Selena, and more!

The crew has a special message for you:

Remember, every astronaut has storms, messes, and tricky missions, but with practice, patience, and your powerful brain, you can steer your ship through anything.

Keep breathing. Keep noticing. Keep exploring.

Well done astronaut!

Mission Complete Checklist

Astronaut Name: ____________________

Mission Code: ADHD Discovery Journey

Date of Graduation: ____________________

What I Discovered on My Journey:

✓ My brain works best when I:

____

____

✓ When I start to feel frustrated, I can:

____

____

✓ When my brain gets distracted, I can:

____

____

✓ Something that helps me calm my rocket is:

____

✓ One thing I'm proud I learned on this mission is:

____

____

____

My Super Skills

Let's reflect on your journey...
Circle any point that sounds like you:

- Staying calm under pressure
- Trying again when things are hard
- Using kind self-talk
- Asking for help when I need it
- Remembering my tools before I react

My Favourite Mission Moment

Draw or describe your favourite activity, challenge, or character from your training:

DEAR PARENT OR CAREGIVER

Your child has just travelled through a universe of learning.

This part is for you.

Your child is not broken or behind.

They have a brain wired for curiosity, creativity, movement, and big feelings.

Brains with ADHD often work like fast rockets; bright and imaginative,

but sometimes challenged by things like sitting still, following long instructions,

switching tasks, or managing frustration.

These challenges are not character flaws.

They are part of how the brain works.

What helps most is predictability, movement, and connection.

Routines and visuals help the brain feel safe.

Movement helps focus and regulation.

Connection before correction helps children feel understood, and that's when

learning happens.

Big feelings are common.
So is worry or overwhelm.
Naming emotions, practicing calming tools, and staying steady together
teaches an important truth:
Regulation is a skill, not a switch.
Focus and motivation work differently, too.
Attention is often interest-based,
not effort-based.
Tools like timers, checklists, breaks, and small rewards can help.
And through it all, your role matters.
You are your child's
anchor, guide, calm center, and safe home base.
Your understanding builds their confidence.
Your patience becomes their courage.
Your belief becomes their spark.

DISCLAIMER:

This book is for educational purposes only. It is not a medical, psychological, or therapeutic treatment, and it should not be used as a substitute for professional advice, diagnosis, or care from a qualified healthcare provider. Every child is unique. If you have concerns about your child's behaviour, learning, emotions, or development, please speak with a licensed doctor, psychologist, counsellor, or other qualified professional.

The strategies, activities, and stories in this book are intended to support learning, self-awareness, and skill-building, but they are not medical recommendations, nor do they replace individualized assessment or treatment.

The author and publisher are not responsible for any actions taken based on the information in this book.

Use your best judgement, follow safety guidelines, and consult a professional when needed.

Meet The Author

Meet Vanessa Fata a wife, mother of two little astronauts, counsellor, and former aesthetics business owner who has always navigated life with a bright, creative, ADHD brain.

Growing up undiagnosed, school often felt like flying through an asteroid field. It wasn't until college, when she finally discovered subjects she loved, that she learned how to use focus tools that helped her thrive.

Before becoming a counsellor, Vanessa poured her creativity into running her own aesthetics business. That same passion, artistry, and eye for detail now fuel her work supporting families and creating engaging tools for children.

As a parent, Vanessa hopes her children (and all children!) learn much earlier that their brains aren't "too busy", but that they're brilliantly wired for imagination, curiosity, and adventure.

One of the biggest lessons she learned is that an ADHD brain may never be quiet, but with the right supports, it can do extraordinary things. In fact, her hyperfocus and spark of dopamine-fueled creativity helped her write this very book.

Vanessa hopes this interactive mission manual helps families feel seen, supported, and empowered as they explore the galaxy of ADHD—together.

Made in United States
North Haven, CT
04 November 2026

21730359R10083